DISCIPLESHIP|EXPLORED

WHAT'S THE BEST LOVE
YOU'VE EVER KNOWN?

HANDBOOK

Discipleship Explored Handbook (3rd Edition)
Copyright © 2018 Christianity Explored. Reprinted in 2018 (three times), 2019.
www.discipleship.explo.red

Published by:
The Good Book Company Ltd
Blenheim House, 1 Blenheim Road, Epsom, Surrey, KT19 9AP, UK
Tel: 0333 123 0880; International: +44 (0) 208 942 0880
Email: info@thegoodbook.co.uk

Websites:
UK and Europe: www.thegoodbook.co.uk
North America: www.thegoodbook.com
Australia: www.thegoodbook.com.au
New Zealand: www.thegoodbook.co.nz

CHRISTIANITY
EXPLORED
MINISTRIES

ISBN: 9781784982027 | Printed in Turkey

Design by André Parker

CONTENTS

WELCOME TO
DISCIPLESHIP|EXPLORED

The word "disciple" means "follower" or "learner."

A disciple of Jesus isn't some kind of super-Christian. In fact, Jesus assumes that all of his followers are disciples.

Over the next eight sessions, we'll be exploring a letter written to some of the earliest Christian disciples by one of the earliest Christian leaders: Paul. He was in chains at the time, guarded day and night by a Roman soldier – and yet, as he keeps telling them, he's overflowing with joy.

We're about to discover why.

Key

≡ Discuss

▷ Watch a film

📖 Read a Bible passage

↑ Pray

SESSION 1
CONFIDENT IN CHRIST

▷ **Confident in Christ** (Philippians 1:1-11)

How can I be confident that I really am a follower of Jesus?

▷ Confident in Christ

- God in his goodness is completely in control of everything – not just when things are going the way we want, but also when they aren't.

- We see this played out as Jesus was dying on the cross: the greatest imaginable good was being achieved by God even when human beings were doing their very worst.

- Because God is in control, we can be confident that nothing can prevent him from completing the good work he has begun in every believer (Philippians 1:6).

- We can be confident that God is working to change us internally if our lives start to reflect this externally.

- Because God is at work in us, we won't be passive. We'll want to respond by growing in our knowledge and love of him (Philippians 1:9-11).

Christ (v 1) | A title meaning "God's anointed one." Sometimes translated as Messiah.
God's holy people (v 1) | Those who God has set apart for himself. This is often translated as "saints." Every follower of Jesus is a saint. The collective description for God's holy people is the "church" (see Philippians 3:6 and 4:15).

Overseers and deacons (v 1) | Church leaders (1 Timothy 3:1-13).
Grace (v 2) | God's goodness to people who do not deserve it.
Gospel (v 5, 7) | The good news that Jesus Christ lived, died, was resurrected, and ascended so that we can be reconciled to God and enjoy him forever.

Day of Christ (v 6, 10) | The day when Jesus Christ will return to judge the world.
Righteousness (v 11) | Perfect goodness. To be righteous is to be "pure and blameless" (v 10).

Righteousness can only come "through Jesus Christ" because only he – as God come to earth – has lived a perfectly pure and blameless life.

📖 **Philippians 1:1-11**

💬 **1. According to Philippians 1:6, what is Paul confident about?**

2. How can he be so confident? (See verse 5.)

3. What do you think that phrase means, in practical terms? (See Philippians 2:25 and 4:14-16.)

4. So how can we be confident that God is working in us? What might that look like in your life and in your day-to-day relationships?

5. Someone might say, "If God will finish this work he started, why do I need to do anything?" What would you say to them?

6. A Christian friend is going through a tough time. They don't feel confident that God loves them and is in control of what is happening to them. Is there something from the film or our discussion that might encourage them?

7. (If time) **What has been most striking for you during this session?**

Follow Up: Paul is confident in Philippians 1:6 that God will complete the "good work" that he began in the Philippians. This "good work" is salvation. The Follow Up activities this week focus on how we can be confident of salvation.

Sunday: Think over what you heard in church this week. What did you find most helpful?

Day 1: Philippians 1:1-11 (Most Bibles have a contents page at the start to help you find particular books.)

If you can, memorize this key verse:
"He who began a good work in you will carry it on to completion until the day of Christ Jesus." (Philippians 1:6)

Day 2: Ephesians 2:8-10

1. Look at verse 8. How are Christians saved?

2. Can Christians save themselves? Why or why not? (See verses 8 and 9.)

3. What cannot save us? (See verse 9.)

4. Are "good works" (i.e. doing good things / not doing bad things) still important for us to do? (See verse 10.)

If you're a Christian, thank God that he has given you the "gift" of faith (verse 8). Praise him for his amazing grace. Ask your Father for growing confidence in him, rather than in your own "works."

When you pray, one helpful model to have in mind is ACTS: **Adoration** (praising God for who he is), **Confession** (speaking honestly about what we've done wrong), **Thanksgiving** (expressing gratitude for all God is doing in your life), and **Supplication** (this is what Paul means in Philippians 4:6 when he says, "Present your requests to God").

Day 3: *"I am the way and the truth and the life. No one comes to the Father except through me."* (Jesus, speaking in John 14:6)

Think about what this verse means for you. Try to memorize it if you can.

Day 4: Read Jesus' words in John 10:27-28.

In this part of John's Gospel, Jesus describes himself as "the good shepherd," and his followers are described as his "sheep."

1. In verse 27, how do "sheep" respond to Jesus?

2. Look at verse 28. What will Jesus give to those who follow him?

3. How confident can we be of salvation, if we follow Jesus? (See verse 28.)

4. Look at verse 27. What is it about us that shows we are followers of Jesus?

Thank God for this stunning promise: "No one will snatch them out of my hand" (verse 28). If we belong to Christ, we can be sure of our salvation. We can trust him completely. He is stronger than anything or anyone else, and he will not let us go.

Day 5: Re-read the passages you've read this week. Pick a verse you found particularly helpful and write it down below.

Day 6: Get ready for *Discipleship Explored* by reading Philippians 1:12-26.

SESSION 2
LIVING IN CHRIST

≋ **Follow Up review**

▷ **Living in Christ** (Philippians 1:12-26)

How was Paul able to be so joyful?

▷ Living in Christ

- While writing to the Philippians, Paul is under house arrest in Rome, people are trying to stir up trouble for him, and he doesn't know if he will live or die.

- And yet Paul can rejoice, because he knows that everything that's happening is actually advancing the gospel (Philippians 1:12). God is in control.

- For Paul, life is about knowing Jesus better and telling others about him.

- Because of that, even death is "gain" for Paul, because then he will "be with Christ, which is better by far" (Philippians 1:23).

- If your greatest joy in life is Jesus Christ, then nothing – not even death – can take your joy away from you.

Brothers and sisters (v 12, 14) | Christians. All Christians are part of God's family.

The Spirit of Jesus Christ (v 19) | The Holy Spirit. God sends his Spirit to help people who become Christians.

📖 **Philippians 1:12-26**

💬 1. Paul is torn between two extremes. What are they?
  (See verses 23-24.)

2. Why is it so hard for him to choose between the two?
  (See verses 22-26.)

3. Paul's life is full of hardship, but he is full of joy (verse
  18). How is that possible?

4. Can you imagine how it would feel to be that joyful? If
  you don't feel that kind of joy, what do you think may be
  keeping you from rejoicing the way Paul does?

5. If your friends were to finish this sentence for you, what do you think they'd say about you: "For them, to live is _____"?

6. Given what we've learned about the source of Paul's unshakable joy, are there any changes you might make in your Christian life this week?

7. (If time) **What has been most striking for you during this session?**

Follow Up: In Philippians 1:19, Paul tells the Philippians that he has been helped by their prayers and "the Spirit of Jesus Christ." This week's Follow Up activities tell us more about the Holy Spirit and what he does.

Sunday: Think over what you heard in church this week. What did you find most helpful?

Day 1: Philippians 1:12-26

If you can, memorize this key verse:
"To live is Christ and to die is gain." (Philippians 1:21)

Day 2: Ephesians 1:13-14

1. When do Christians receive the Holy Spirit? (See verse 13.)

2. What does the Holy Spirit guarantee? (See verse 14.)

3. How will that truth affect your feelings, day to day, even when things are tough?

Thank God that the Holy Spirit's presence in us guarantees that we belong to him.

Day 3: *"If you love me, keep my commands. And I will ask the Father, and he will give you another advocate to help you and be with you forever – the Spirit of truth. The world cannot accept him, because it neither sees him nor knows him. But you know him, for he lives with you and will be in you. I will not leave you as orphans; I will come to you."* (Jesus, speaking in John 14:15-18)

Thank God that if you love Jesus, you're never alone. His Spirit lives with you and in you. And he promises never to leave you.

Day 4: Galatians 5:16-23

Paul explains that inside every Christian there's a fight going on: between our sinful nature and the Holy Spirit.

1. Look at verse 16. What does it mean to "live by the Spirit"?

2. Looking at verses 19-21, is there anything mentioned here that you need to turn from, with the Spirit's help?

3. Looking at verses 22-23, are there ways in which you can grow, with the Spirit's help?

Thank God for the Holy Spirit, who gives us the power to live in the way Paul describes. Because of the Spirit, we're no longer enslaved to sin. We are free to love God and others joyfully.

Day 5: Re-read the passages you've read this week. Pick a verse you found particularly helpful and write it down below.

Day 6: Get ready for *Discipleship Explored* by reading Philippians 1:27 – 2:11.

SESSION 3
ONE IN CHRIST

🗨 **Follow Up review**

▷ **One in Christ** (Philippians 1:27 – 2:11)

What are the biggest threats to our unity with each other?

▷ One in Christ

- Paul repeatedly writes about *koinonia*. This Greek word means unity, partnership, or togetherness with one another.

- When we love the brothers and sisters in our local church, it shows that we really are followers of Jesus. It also shows the world that the gospel is true and powerful (Philippians 1:27-28; John 13:35).

- But our unity is under threat by opposition from outside the church (Philippians 1:28).

- Opposition can be frightening. But like faith itself, suffering for Christ is a gift from God (Philippians 1:29). It makes us more like Jesus, and proves that we are "co-heirs" with him (Romans 8:17).

- Our unity is also under threat because of pride from inside the church (Philippians 2:3).

- Our pride is shattered if we consider the humility of Jesus. He came from the highest place, yet made himself the lowest: a slave who came to serve others by dying for them on a cross (Philippians 2:5-8).

- So in that spirit of humility, will we love and serve each other in our local church – and be of one mind with each other (Philippians 2:2)?

The gospel of Christ (v 27) | The good news about Jesus Christ.

The one Spirit (v 27) | The Holy Spirit. God gives his Spirit to all Christians.

📖 **Philippians 1:27 – 2:11**

💬 **1. In Philippians 1:27, Paul says we should conduct ourselves "in a manner worthy of the gospel." According to Philippians 1:27 and 2:2, what does this look like?**

2. Paul wants us to be "striving together as one for the faith of the gospel" (verse 27). What does that involve? (See Philippians 1:7, 14, 27.)

3. Where does this oneness come from? (See Philippians 2:1.)

4. Jesus commanded believers to love each other: "By this everyone will know that you are my disciples, if you love one another" (John 13:35). What might you say to a friend who said, "I love Jesus but I don't like going to church"?

5. In Philippians 2:3, Paul says, "Do nothing out of selfish ambition and vain conceit. Rather, in humility value others above yourselves..." Why do you think pride is such a threat to church unity?

6. If even God the Son made himself "nothing" (2:7), how much more should we – as his creatures! – make ourselves nothing in the service of others? In what ways can we do that this week at our church?

7. (If time) **What has been most striking for you during this session?**

Follow Up: In Philippians 1:27, Paul encourages followers of Jesus to "stand firm in the one Spirit, striving together as one." It's vital that we meet regularly with other believers. This week's Follow Up activities focus on that theme.

Sunday: Think over what you heard in church this week. What did you find most helpful?

Day 1: Philippians 1:27 – 2:11

If you can, memorize this key verse:
"Stand firm in the one Spirit, striving together as one for the faith of the gospel." (Philippians 1:27)

📖 **Day 2: Colossians 3:12-17**

1. When "God's chosen people" meet together (verse 12), how should we treat each other? (See verses 12-14.)

2. Look at verse 13. Why must we forgive one another?

3. Where do you think we can find "the message of Christ" (verse 16)? Practically speaking, how can we "let the message of Christ dwell" in us?

4. Paul says that thankfulness and gratitude for what Christ has done is very important. He mentions it three times (verses 15, 16, and 17). Write down what Christ has done for you, and give thanks to him.

Our witness to a watching world is even more powerful when they see how we love each other. Pray that God would give you a deep love for the people in your church.

Day 3: *"And let us consider how we may spur one another on toward love and good deeds, not giving up meeting together, as some are in the habit of doing, but encouraging one another – and all the more as you see the Day approaching."* (Hebrews 10:24-25)

Think of one way you can encourage a fellow believer toward love and good deeds, and do it this week. Ask God to give you strength, by his Holy Spirit, so that you can be an encouragement to a Christian brother or sister in your local church.

Day 4: 1 Peter 2:9-12

1. How does Peter describe Christians in verses 9 and 10?

2. What should Christians be doing together as a result of these descriptions? (See verse 9.)

3. Why does Peter describe Christians as "foreigners and exiles" in verse 11? (See Philippians 3:20 for a clue!)

4. Look at verses 11 and 12. How should "the people of God" behave?

5. What will be the effect when people see Christians living in this way? (See verse 12.)

Spend some time reflecting on your new status in Christ (verses 9-11). Thank God for these amazing truths. Ask him to give you Christian friends who can help you live a life in keeping with God's chosen people.

Day 5: Re-read the passages you've read this week. Pick a verse you found particularly helpful and write it down below.

Day 6: Get ready for *Discipleship Explored* by reading Philippians 2:12-30.

SESSION 4
OBEDIENT IN CHRIST

💬 **Follow Up review**

▷ **Obedient in Christ** (Philippians 2:12-30)

If God forgives all my sin, why does it matter how I live?

▷ Obedient in Christ

- Just as Jesus obeyed his Father, so we must obey our Father too.

- This obedience mustn't be an attempt to earn our salvation. Jesus has already earned it for us. Paul says, "Work *out* your salvation" (Philippians 2:12), not "Work *for* your salvation."

- "Religion says, 'I obey, therefore I'm accepted.' Christianity says, 'I'm accepted, *therefore* I obey.'"

- "Working out your salvation" means acting in line with your salvation. It means obeying Christ.

- Living obediently will make us "shine ... like stars" (Philippians 2:15), so that others might be attracted to Christ.

- We should be disciple-making disciples. Real disciples of Jesus want to tell others about him. As Jesus said, "The mouth speaks what the heart is full of" (Luke 6:45).

The word of life (v 16) | The word of life is Scripture; God's word; the good news about Jesus. In 1 John 1:1, Jesus is described as "the Word of life."
The day of Christ (v 16) | The day when Jesus Christ will return to judge the world.

Drink offering ... sacrifice (v 17) | In Old Testament times, an offering of wine or water was poured on top of an animal sacrifice presented to God. Paul imagines his life as a "drink offering" poured out on top of the Philippians' sacrificial service of others.

📖 **Philippians 2:12-30**

💬 1. Someone might say, "Jesus forgives all my sin – past, present, and future. So it doesn't really matter how I live." What would Paul say to them, based on Philippians 2:12?

2. Why do we do this "with fear and trembling"? (See verse 13.)

3. What is it that enables us to shine "like stars in the sky," according to verses 14-16?

4. Why do you think Paul talks about his friends Timothy and Epaphroditus here in verses 19-30? How do they shine like stars?

5. Jesus commanded his followers to "go and make disciples of all nations" (Matthew 28:19). He also said, "The mouth speaks what the heart is full of" (Luke 6:45). How does the second quote help us obey the first?

6. This week, what are some practical ways we can fill our hearts with Jesus Christ so that we can help to "make disciples" of others?

7. (If time) **What has been most striking for you during this session?**

Follow Up: In Philippians 2:16, Paul tells the Philippians to "hold firmly to the word of life." As we hear and obey God's word, we become more like Christ. This week's Follow Up activities focus on the theme of the Bible.

Sunday: Think over what you heard in church this week. What did you find most helpful?

Day 1: Philippians 2:12-30

If you can, memorize this key verse:
"Continue to work out your salvation with fear and trembling, for it is God who works in you to will and to act in order to fulfill his good purpose." (Philippians 2:12-13)

Day 2: 2 Timothy 3:14-17

Here, Paul is writing to Timothy, the younger evangelist who helped him start the church in Philippi.

1. Look at verse 15. What are the "Holy Scriptures" able to do?

2. Paul wrote these words to Timothy. But where does Scripture ultimately come from? (See verse 16.)

3. What does Scripture equip a Christian to do? (See verse 16.)

4. Look at verse 17. Why should we read the Bible?

Thank God that he reveals himself to you through his word. Ask him to help you know him better each day, and to be excited by the things he shows you as you read the word he has breathed out.

📖 **Day 3:** *"Your word is a lamp for my feet, a light on my path."* (Psalm 119:105)

God's word guides us, and makes us wise. It helps us know the right choices to make, and the right way to think and live. Ask God to help you trust it more and more over the coming months.

📖 **Day 4: Psalm 19:7-8**

This psalm was written by David, a famous king of Israel, hundreds of years before Jesus was born.

1. **What words are used to describe "the law/statutes of the Lord" (God's word) in verse 7?**

2. **What effect will God's word have on us if we read it? (See verse 7.)**

3. What words are used to describe God's word in verse 8?

4. How will God's word impact us if we read and obey it? (See verse 8.)

Read the rest of Psalm 19, and notice all the wonderful ways in which God's word is described. Use the words of the psalm to pray your own prayer.

Day 5: Re-read the passages you've read this week. Pick a verse you found particularly helpful and write it down below.

Day 6: Get ready for *Discipleship Explored* by reading Philippians 3:1-9.

SESSION 5
RIGHTEOUS IN CHRIST

≣ **Follow Up review**

▷ **Righteous in Christ** (Philippians 3:1-9)

What's wrong with our righteousness?

▷ Righteous in Christ

- Many people, even Christians, think that God will accept them because of the good things they do, or the bad things they don't do.

- But Christianity says God accepts us because of what *Christ* has done.

- Religiously speaking, Paul had done everything right (Philippians 3:5-6).

- But now that he knows Jesus and his perfect righteousness, Paul realizes that all of his "righteousness" is actually "garbage" (Philippians 3:8).

- We desperately need a righteousness that is not our own, but comes from God. We can only get that righteousness by faith in God's Son, Jesus Christ.

- That's because he – and he alone – lived the life we should have lived. And then he – and he alone – died the death we deserve to die.

- We must "watch out" (Philippians 3:2). If we think God will accept us because of the good things we've done, we treat our Creator as if he's in our debt.

Circumcision/circumcised (v 3, 5) | For Jewish people, this is a sign that a man is one of God's people. Some taught that circumcision is necessary for a Christian to be acceptable to God, but Paul knows only Christ is necessary.
God ... Spirit ... Christ Jesus (v 3) | Scripture reveals God to be three "persons" in one: God the Father, God the Son (Jesus Christ), and God the Spirit.
Tribe of Benjamin (v 5) | All Jews came from one of twelve tribes. Benjamin was one of only two tribes that kept following God in the Old Testament.
Hebrew (v 5) | Another word for a Jewish person.
Pharisees (v 5) | A group of Jews who followed religious rules and customs very strictly.

Philippians 3:1-9

1. Paul lists his impressive religious qualifications in Philippians 3:5-6. What similar things do people today think will make them acceptable to God?

2. What is Paul's view of those religious qualifications now? (See verses 7 and 8.)

3. Paul no longer puts any confidence in who he is or what he has done. According to verse 8, who is he placing his confidence in now – and why?

4. What does it mean for us as followers of Jesus to "consider everything a loss" (verse 8)? (See Luke 14:33.)

5. What kind of righteousness has Paul now gained, according to verse 9?

6. How can you and I get this righteousness? (See verse 9.)

7. (If time) **What has been most striking for you during this session?**

↪**Follow Up:** In Philippians 3:9, Paul speaks about "the righteousness that comes from God on the basis of faith." This week's Follow Up activities focus on the theme of righteousness.

🗨 **Sunday:** Think over what you heard in church this week. What did you find most helpful?

📖 **Day 1: Philippians 3:1-9**

If you can, memorize this key verse:
"*Not having a righteousness of my own that comes from the law, but that which is through faith in Christ.*" (Philippians 3:9)

📖 Day 2: Romans 3:20-24

In this passage, "declared righteous in God's sight" (verse 20) means "made right with God." "The law" (verse 20) means God's law, the Ten Commandments.

1. Look at verse 20. What does "the law" do?

2. If the law can't make us righteous in God's sight (verse 20), how can we be made righteous? (See verse 22.)

3. How is that made possible? (See verse 24.)

God does not leave our sin unpunished: it was paid for by Jesus when he died in our place. Because of what happened at the cross, God forgives his people their sin, and gives them the righteousness of Jesus.

Spend some time reflecting on the wonder of this. Thank God that all who repent and believe in Jesus "are justified freely by his grace" (verse 24).

Day 3: *"God made him who had no sin to be sin for us, so that in him we might become the righteousness of God."* (2 Corinthians 5:21)

In other words, Jesus took all our sin – even our very worst sins – on himself when he died. Jesus received the condemnation we deserve, so that we would never have to. Those who are "in him" now have his righteousness. Praise and thank God for his amazing love!

Day 4: Romans 5:6-10

1. **Look at verses 6-8. What is so amazing about Christ's death?**

2. **What does that prove about God's attitude toward us? (See verse 8.)**

3. What has Jesus' death achieved for us, according to verses 9 and 10?

Reflect on your answer to the last question. If you're a follower of Jesus, all these things are true for you. Allow these truths to sink in and move you to worship. Pray, thanking God for all he has done for you.

Day 5: Re-read the passages you've read this week. Pick a verse you found particularly helpful and write it down below.

Day 6: Get ready for *Discipleship Explored* by reading Philippians 3:10-21.

SESSION 6
TRANSFORMED
IN CHRIST

≡ **Follow Up review**

▷ **Transformed in Christ** (Philippians 3:10-21)

How can we become more like Christ?

▷ Transformed in Christ

- Jesus is more valuable to Paul than anything. Paul wants to do whatever it takes to know Jesus better and become more like him (Philippians 3:10-11).

- One of the ways we can become more like Christ is by imitating godly believers (Philippians 3:17).

- Another way in which we become more like Christ is through suffering (Philippians 3:10).

- Christ will one day return, and on that day he "will transform our lowly bodies so that they will be like his glorious body" (Philippians 3:21).

- Paul's picture of discipleship is not passive but active. We're to be like an athlete running a race, "forgetting what is behind and straining toward what is ahead" (Philippians 3:13).

- Sometimes regrets over "what is behind" can hold us back – and Paul had many reasons to regret his past.

- But believers can forget what is behind because we know that we are forgiven, and everything in our past is ultimately intended by God to make us more like Christ.

Attaining to the resurrection (v 11) | Being raised to life by Christ after death.

📖 Philippians 3:10-21

💬 1. What's the one thing Paul does (according to verses 13-14), and why does he do it?

2. What are Paul's "goal" and "prize"? (See verses 10-11.)

3. Some might say that Christianity is just about avoiding hell and going to heaven. Given verses 10-14, what do you think Paul would say to that?

4. In verses 18-19, Paul writes "with tears" about enemies of Christ. As well as the more obvious "enemies," this group can include those who claim to be Christian teachers but are not. How can we identify such people (see verses 18-19)?

5. What are the sharp contrasts between the enemies of Christ in verse 19 and the disciples of Christ in verses 20-21?

6. This week, how can we "press on toward the goal" (verse 14) of knowing Christ and becoming more like him?

7. (If time) **What has been most striking for you during this session?**

Follow Up: In Philippians 3:10, Paul speaks about his strong desire to "know Christ" and become more like him. He knows that this means he must "press on toward the goal to win the prize" (3:14). This week's Follow Up activities will help you think about what it means to "press on" and know Christ better.

Sunday: Think over what you heard in church this week. What did you find most helpful?

Day 1: Philippians 3:10-21

If you can, memorize this key verse:
"I want to know Christ." (Philippians 3:10)

Day 2: Matthew 6:19-24

1. Jesus tells us to store up "treasures in heaven" rather than "treasures on earth." Why? (See verses 19-20.)

2. Look at Jesus' words in verse 21. How might we be able to tell what we really value in life?

3. How do you use most of your time and energy? What does this show about where your heart is?

4. In verse 24, Jesus says that no one can serve two masters. What are the things in your life that keep you from knowing Christ better?

When Jesus says, "Store up for yourselves treasures in heaven," he is telling us to live wholeheartedly for him. There's an old poem that helps explain why this is the best way to live:

> "Only one life, 'twill soon be past.
> Only what's done for Christ will last."

Ask your Father to help you live for things that will last.

Day 3: *"If anyone is in Christ, the new creation has come: The old has gone, the new is here!"* (2 Corinthians 5:17)

The Christian life can be summed up in four words: "Be who you are!" Or, to put it another way, "You are now in Christ – act like it!"

Ask God for power to live a life that is more like Christ's.

Day 4: Matthew 7:24-27

1. There are two men in this story. How does Jesus describe their characters? (See verses 24 and 26.)

2. The men both built houses, but differently. What was different about the way they built? (See verses 24 and 26.)

3. What happened to each man's house when the storm hit? (See verses 25 and 27.)

4. Why isn't it enough just to hear Jesus' words? (See verses 26-27; see also Matthew 7:21-23.)

Many people go to church or say they are Christian, but they don't really know Christ. The mark of a genuine believer is whether or not we put God's word into practice. Only then will we be transformed more and more into the likeness of Christ.

Ask God by his Spirit to make you a person who treats Jesus not only as Savior, but also as Lord over every part of your life.

Day 5: Re-read the passages you've read this week. Pick a verse you found particularly helpful and write it down below.

Day 6: Get ready for *Discipleship Explored* by reading Philippians 4:1-9.

SESSION 7
REJOICING IN CHRIST

≡ **Follow Up review**

▷ **Rejoicing in Christ** (Philippians 4:1-9)

What should we remember if we're in conflict with another believer?

▷ Rejoicing in Christ

- Euodia and Syntyche were two Philippian believers who were in sharp disagreement with each other.

- Paul pleads with them to "be of the same mind in the Lord" (Philippians 4:2).

- That phrase, "in the Lord" or "in Christ," is key to understanding how we can be united with each other and "rejoice" (Philippians 4:4).

- The phrase "in Christ" reminds believers that we are completely united with Christ. All that is his is ours.

- Not only are we "in Christ," but he – by his Spirit – is in us.

- Remembering how rich we are in Christ means we no longer have to scrabble around after the "pennies" of approval, or power, or recognition, or getting our own way.

- We also have the privilege of praying "in Christ." The way to be anxious about nothing is to be prayerful about everything (Philippians 4:6-7).

Whose names are in the book of life (v 3) | A way of saying that these people are saved. They are genuine followers of Jesus.

Philippians 4:1-9

1. Why do you think people tend to quarrel with one another?

2. If those are the reasons why we quarrel with each other, how does it help to remember that we're "in the Lord" (verses 1, 2, 4)?

3. Why will remembering that "the Lord is near" (verse 5) make us gentle with others?

4. What action should we take when we're anxious? When should we do it, and why? (See verses 6-7.)

5. How will praying in that way make us feel like rejoicing "in the Lord"?

6. Read verses 8-9. How can we put these verses into practice this week?

7. (If time) **What has been most striking for you during this session?**

Follow Up: In Philippians 4:6, Paul says, "Do not be anxious about anything, but in every situation, by prayer and petition, with thanksgiving, present your requests to God." There's a close connection between how much we pray and how much we rejoice. So this week's Follow Up activities focus on prayer.

Sunday: Think over what you heard in church this week. What did you find most helpful?

Day 1: Philippians 4:1-9

If you can, memorize this key verse:
"Rejoice in the Lord always. I will say it again: Rejoice!"
(Philippians 4:4)

Day 2: Colossians 1:3-14

In this passage, Paul prays for the Christians living in a place called Colossae.

1. **What emotion does Paul express as he prays for these Christians? (See verse 3. Clue: He feels the same way when he prays in Philippians 1:3-4.)**

2. Look at verse 9. How often does Paul pray for the Colossians?

3. What does Paul pray for the Colossians? (See verses 9-10.)

4. What can you learn from Paul about how to pray for yourself and others?

None of Paul's prayers for his friends contain an appeal for God to change their circumstances. Could there be a lesson for us here? As you pray now, put into practice what you've just learned from the way Paul prays.

Day 3: *"If you, then, though you are evil, know how to give good gifts to your children, how much more will your Father in heaven give good gifts to those who ask him!"* (Jesus, speaking in Matthew 7:11)

Jesus says that even a sinful, earthly father knows how to give good gifts to his children. Imagine, then, how much more your perfect Father in heaven will give his children good gifts if they ask him!

Ask your Father for whatever "good gifts" you need. Remember that what we want is not always what we need. If you have not been given something you want – even desperately want to the extent of feeling that you need it – your loving Father has something better in mind for you.

"Everything is needful that he sends; nothing can be needful that he withholds." (John Newton)

Day 4: Matthew 6:5-13

In this passage, Jesus himself teaches his disciples how they should pray.

1. What kinds of things should we avoid when we pray? (See verses 5-8.)

2. Look at verses 9-10. What is the first thing Jesus tells the disciples to do as they pray? (Note: "Hallowed" means "highly honored.")

3. How different is this from the way that you usually pray?

4. In verses 11-13, Jesus teaches us to pray for three things in particular. What are they?

**5. If "your Father knows what you need before you ask him"
(Matthew 6:8), why do you think Jesus tells us to pray?**

Pray now, rejoicing that your Father in heaven hears you and loves to hear your prayers.

Day 5: Re-read the passages you've read this week. Pick a verse you found particularly helpful and write it down below.

Day 6: Get ready for *Discipleship Explored* by reading Philippians 4:10-23.

SESSION 8
CONTENT IN CHRIST

 Follow Up review

 Content in Christ (Philippians 4:10-23)

What's the secret of contentment?

(▷) **Content in Christ**

- What is the one thing you feel you lack that would finally bring you contentment?

- Paul knew that deep contentment can be experienced regardless of how much we have or how little (Philippians 4:11-12) – because it's found in Christ (Philippians 4:13).

- The Philippians understood how "rich" they were in Christ, and this awareness enabled them to support Paul generously and self-sacrificially (Philippians 4:14-16).

- They also knew from their own experience that "it is more blessed to give than to receive" (Acts 20:35).

- We'll finally discover the secret of contentment when we become "like a weaned child" (Psalm 131:2) – always trusting our Father completely even though, like a child, we won't always understand everything he does.

- Lasting contentment only comes when we've learned to trust that our Father holds us in his arms, intends everything – even our suffering – for our good, and will meet our deepest needs "in Christ Jesus" (Philippians 4:19).

Macedonia (v 15) | Philippi was in Macedonia, part of ancient Greece. See map on page 79.
Thessalonica (v 16) | Another city in Macedonia.

Amen (v 20, 23) | A Hebrew word meaning "truth" and "certainty." The word "amen" confirms that what has just been spoken is true.

📖 Philippians 4:10-23

💬 1. If you're being honest, how would you finish this sentence: "I can be content, as long as _____ "?

2. If we currently feel discontent, what would Paul say to encourage us? (See Philippians 4:11-12.)

3. Where does Paul find true contentment, according to Philippians 4:13? (See also 1:21, 3:10-11 and 4:7.)

4. Paul is in chains as he writes. He's been "hungry" and "in want," and has had many "troubles" (4:12, 14). Yet he is content in Christ. Briefly skim through Philippians to find some of the things that make this possible.

5. Which of these realities do you most struggle to believe?

6. Now that *Discipleship Explored* is finished, what steps would you like to take next? Are there any resolutions you'd like to make, or is there anything your brothers and sisters in Christ could help you with?

7. (If time) **What has been most striking for you during this session?**

Follow Up: Paul ends his letter to the Philippians by speaking about contentment. He says, "I have learned to be content whatever the circumstances" (Philippians 4:11) – and this comes from a man who is in chains! As we reach the end of *Discipleship Explored*, the Follow Up activities this week focus on how we can remain content, even in difficult circumstances.

Sunday: Think over what you heard in church this week. What did you find most helpful?

Day 1: Philippians 4:10-23

If you can, memorize this key verse:
"I have learned the secret of being content in any and every situation." (Philippians 4:12)

Day 2: 1 Timothy 6:6-12

Paul is writing to Timothy, the younger evangelist who helped him start the church in Philippi.

1. Paul says, "Godliness with contentment is great gain. For we brought nothing into the world, and we can take nothing out of it" (verses 6-7). Are you living for something that you can't take with you? How might that affect your contentment?

2. Look at verses 9-10. What else might keep us from being content?

3. What should we do instead, if we want to be content? (See verses 11-12.)

It's very hard to just stop loving money and earthly things. Desire for those things needs to be driven out by love for something – or someone – greater.

Ask God to give you a love for Jesus that is more powerful than your love for earthly things. Ask him to open your eyes so that you can see how much more desirable Christ is than anything else.

Day 3: *"Follow God's example, therefore, as dearly loved children and walk in the way of love, just as Christ loved us and gave himself up for us as a fragrant offering and sacrifice to God."* (Ephesians 5:1-2)

Following Christ means following his lead in every area of your life. Ask your Father in heaven for strength to "walk in the way of love," just as your Lord and Savior did.

Day 4: Colossians 3:1-10

Paul says that it's not enough for us to have "taken off" our old selves (verse 9). We must also "put on the new self" (verse 10) if we are to experience the contentment Christ brings.

1. **Paul says, "Set your hearts on things above, where Christ is." In other words, Christians should desire and live for those things that are Christ-like. Why is that? (Look at the beginning of verse 1.)**

2. **What does that mean? (See verse 4.)**

3. How should Christians live in the light of that fact? (See the start of verse 5.)

4. Look at verses 5-10. Make a list of the things Paul tells us to turn away from.

5. What will your "new self" (verse 10) look like? Write down words that are the opposite of the ones you wrote down in question 4.

Your contentment as a Christian will depend on setting your heart on things above (verse 1). Pray that God's Holy Spirit will give you power and self-control to take off the old self and put on the new. Ask your loving Father to give you deep, lasting contentment as you do that.

Day 5: Spend some time looking back over these Follow Up activities. What can you thank God for? In what ways can you ask his Spirit to help you grow?

Pray about these things, thanking him for all he's done for you in Jesus.

Day 6: Philippians 1:9-11 gives you an idea of what Paul, if he were here, might pray for you right at this moment:

"This is my prayer: that your love may abound more and more in knowledge and depth of insight, so that you may be able to discern what is best and may be pure and blameless for the day of Christ, filled with the fruit of righteousness that comes through Jesus Christ – to the glory and praise of God."

So, what happens next?

• Keep reading!

Keep going with your Bible-reading, so that "your love may abound more and more in knowledge and depth of insight." The book of James is a great follow-up to Philippians. Why not start to read that, beginning tomorrow?

• Keep praying!

The most joyful Christians are prayerful Christians, because through prayer we become even closer in our friendship with

Christ. Paul usually begins his letters with a prayer, and the prayers begin with thanks and gratitude for what God has done. That's a great thing for us to copy as we pray.

• Keep meeting!

Keep meeting regularly with other Christians. The Holy Spirit gives every Christian "spiritual gifts." He gives these gifts so that we can strengthen other believers, and so that others can do the same for us (1 Corinthians 12:7). So "stand firm in the one Spirit, striving together as one for the faith of the gospel" (Philippians 1:27). And be encouraged. We're praying for you.

"Finally, brothers and sisters, whatever is true, whatever is noble, whatever is right, whatever is pure, whatever is lovely, whatever is admirable – if anything is excellent or praiseworthy – think about such things. Whatever you have learned or received or heard from me, or seen in me – put it into practice. And the God of peace will be with you." (Philippians 4:8-9)

ABOUT
PHILIPPIANS

Who wrote it?

The apostle Paul wrote the letter to the Philippians.

Where and when was it written?

Philippians 1:13-14 tells us that Paul wrote the letter while "in chains." Most likely, this was the period of his life when he was under house arrest in Rome (Acts 28:14-31). Paul was allowed to live by himself in his own rented house, albeit with a soldier to guard him. He was also free to receive visitors, teaching them about the Lord Jesus Christ "with all boldness and without hindrance!"

The evidence suggests that it was written around AD 61.

Who was he writing to?

Followers of Christ in Philippi, Macedonia (in modern-day Greece). The city of Philippi was a bustling Roman colony whose inhabitants prided themselves on being Roman citizens. Many Philippians made a point of speaking Latin, and even dressed like Romans. This is perhaps why Paul makes a point of stressing, "But our citizenship is in heaven" (Philippians 3:20).

Why was it written?

First and foremost, Paul wrote because he dearly loved the believers in Philippi. He says, "God can testify how I long for all of you with the affection of Christ Jesus" (Philippians 1:8). But Paul also wanted to thank the Philippians for the gift they'd sent via their messenger Epaphroditus, when they found out Paul had been detained (Philippians 4:10, 18).

As he writes, Paul reports on his present circumstances, encourages them to stand firm and rejoice in the face of persecution, urges them to be humble and united, warns them against certain dangerous teachers, and reminds them of the righteousness that is theirs in Christ.

What's distinctive about the letter?

It's been called the New Testament letter of joy. The word "joy," in its various forms, occurs sixteen times in Philippians. It's also the letter of *koinonia*, a Greek word meaning partnership or oneness. See for example Philippians 1:4-5, where Paul writes, "In all my prayers for all of you, I always pray with joy, because of your partnership (*koinonia*) in the gospel from the first day until now..."

Koinonia is a word that stresses how communal the Christian life must be. The word is also used to describe our union with Christ as believers: "Therefore if you have any encouragement from being united with Christ, if any comfort from his love, if any common sharing (*koinonia*) in the Spirit..." (Philippians 2:1). For Paul, *koinonia* with Christ leads to *koinonia* with other believers.

EXTRAS

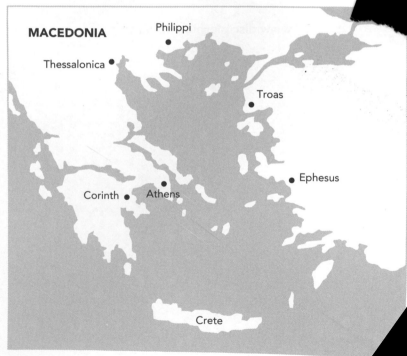

www.discipleship.explo.red